Thinking of You

Thinking of You

MQP

I am always conscious
of my nearness to
you, your presence
never leaves me.

Johann Wolfgang von Goethe

May no gift be too small
to give, nor too simple to
receive, which is wrapped
in thoughtfulness, and
tied with love.

L. O. Baird

Hope is a thing with feathers
That perches in the soul
And sings a tune without words
And never stops at all.

Emily Dickinson

Better by far that you should forget and smile
Than that you should remember and be sad.

Christina Rossetti

To send a letter is a good way
to go somewhere without
moving anything but your heart.

Phyllis Theroux

Food, glorious food!

Lionel Bart

You can kiss your family and friends good-bye and put miles between you, but at the same time you carry them with you in your heart, your mind, your stomach, because you do not just live in a world but a world lives in you.

Frederick Buechner

Life is so short, so fast the lone hours fly,
We ought to be together, you and I.

Henry Alford

If instead of a gem, or even a flower, we should cast the gift of a loving thought into the heart of a friend, that would be giving as the angels give.

George MacDonald

February, when the days
of winter seem endless
and no amount of wistful
recollecting can bring
back any air of summer.

Shirley Jackson

The charm, one might say
the genius of memory, is
that it is choosy, chancy,
and temperamental: it rejects
the edifying cathedral and
indelibly photographs the
small boy outside, chewing
a hunk of melon in the dust.

Elizabeth Bowen

Only three people got out of the 11.54. The first was a countrywoman with two baskety boxes full of live chickens who stuck their russet heads out anxiously through the wicker bars; the second was Miss Peckitt, the grocer's wife's cousin, with a tin box and three brown-paper parcels; and the third—

"Oh! My Daddy, my Daddy!" That scream went like a knife into the heart of everyone in the train, and people put their heads out of the windows to see a tall pale man with lips set in a thin close line, and a little girl clinging to him with arms and legs, while his arms went tightly round her.

E. Nesbit

More than kisses, letters mingle souls.

John Donne

I arise from dreams of thee
In the first sweet sleep of night,
When the winds are breathing low,
And the stars are shining bright.

Percy Bysshe Shelley

She I love is
far away.

Jean-Jacques Rousseau

I had not thought of
   violets of late,
The wild, shy kind that
   springs beneath your feet
In wistful April days.

Alice Dunbar-Nelson

With thee conversing,
  I forget all time,
All seasons, and
  their change.

John Milton

Wish you were here.

No one can look back on his school days and say with truth that they were altogether unhappy.

George Orwell

I am tired, Beloved, of chafing my heart against
The want of you;
Of squeezing it into little inkdrops,
And posting it.

Amy Lowell

Piglet sidled up to Pooh from behind.

"Pooh!" he whispered.

"Yes, Piglet?"

"Nothing," said Piglet, taking Pooh's paw. "I just wanted to be sure of you."

A. A. Milne

Somewhere, there is someone
who dreams of your smile,
who finds in your presence
that life is worthwhile.
So when you are lonely,
remember it's true,
that somebody, somewhere,
is thinking of you.

Author unknown

He never is alone that
is accompanied with
noble thoughts.

John Fletcher

If I had a rose for every time
I thought of you, I'd walk
through a garden forever.

Author unknown

My dearest Angel, I was made happy by the pleasure of receiving your letter of September 19th, and I rejoice to hear that you are so very good a girl, and love my dear Lady Hamilton, who most dearly loves you. Give her a kiss for me.

Lord Nelson

I count myself in nothing else
so happy as in a soul
remembering my good friends.

William Shakespeare

Love reckons hours for months, and days for years; every little absence is an age.

John Dryden

Strephon kissed me in the spring,
Robin in the fall,
But Colin only looked at me
And never kissed at all.

Strephon's kiss was lost in jest,
Robin's lost in play,
But the kiss in Colin's eyes
Haunts me night and day.

Sara Teasdale

We'll talk about
everything. I've
got so much I
want to tell you.

Leo Tolstoy

I have enlarged my life by thoughts of you. Hardly a quarter hour of my waking time passes without me thinking about you, and there are many quarter hours in which I do nothing else.

Franz Kafka

The road goes on forever
and the party never ends.

Robert Earl Keen

When you are sorrowful look again in your heart, and you shall see that in truth you are weeping for that which has been your delight.

Kahlil Gibran

What would not I give to wander
Where my old companions dwell?
Absence makes the heart grow fonder,
Isle of Beauty, fare thee well!

Thomas Haynes Bayly

A letter is a Joy of Earth.

Emily Dickinson

When delicate and feeling souls are separated, there is not a feature in the sky, not a movement of the elements, not an aspiration of the breeze, but hints some cause for a lover's apprehension.

Richard Brinsley Sheridan

They told me, Heraclitus, they told me
    you were dead,
They brought me bitter news to hear
    and bitter tears to shed.
I wept as I remember'd, how often
    you and I
Had tired the sun with talking and
    sent him down the sky.

William Johnson Cory

May the best of your past be the worst of your future.

Author unknown

What was hard to bear is
sweet to remember.

Portuguese proverb

Mother is the name for
God in the lips and
hearts of little children.

William Makepeace Thackeray

My Antony is away.

William Shakespeare

Drink to me only with thine eyes,
And I will pledge with mine;
Or leave a kiss but in the cup,
And I'll not look for wine.

Ben Jonson

Can miles truly separate you from friends…. If you want to be with someone you love, aren't you already there?

Richard Bach

So, either by thy picture or my love,
Thy self away, art present still with me;
For thou not farther than my thoughts canst move,
And I am still with them, and they with thee.

William Shakespeare

Where we love is home—home that our feet may leave, but not our hearts.

Oliver Wendell Holmes

The one good thing
about not seeing
you is that I can
write you letters.

Svetlana Alliluyeva

I dropped a tear in
the ocean. The day
you find it is the day
I will stop missing you.

Author unknown

Oh lovelorn heart, give o'er—
Cause thy vain dreams of beauty's warmth—forget
The face thou longest for.

Meleager of Gadara

Grandfather's been dead for all these years, but if you lifted my skull, by God, in the convolutions of my brain you'd find the big ridges of his thumbprint. He touched me.

Ray Bradbury

If the while I think on
    thee, dear friend,
All losses are restor'd and
    sorrows end.

William Shakespeare

By yon bonnie banks, and by yon bonnie braes
Where the sun shines bright, on Loch Lomond
Oh we two have passed, so many blithesome days,
On the bonnie, bonnie banks O' Loch Lomond.

Oh ye'll take the high road and I'll take the low road,
An' I'll be in Scotland before ye',
But woe is my heart until we meet again
On the bonnie, bonnie banks O' Loch Lomond.

Traditional Scottish song

I like my body when
it is with your
body.

E. E. Cummings

The world is so empty if one thinks only of mountains, rivers and cities; but to know someone who thinks and feels with us, and who, though distant is close to us in spirit, this makes the earth for us an inhabited garden.

Johann Wolfgang von Goethe

Picture Credits

Cover: Spring Flowers, circa 1955. p.5: Lost In The City, 1954. p.6: Present From Daddy, 1944. p.9: Fascinating Globe, circa 1950. p.10: Dream On, 1957. p.13: Posting A Letter, 1936. p.15: If Only, circa 1945, © Camerique/Getty Images. p.16: Adoring Mary, 1937, © Paramount Pictures/Getty Images. p.19: I'll Start Again, circa 1945, © Lambert/Getty Images. p.20: Fairy Clock, 1949. p.23: Blackpool Sands, circa 1956. p.24: Family Album, 1947. p.26: Leaving Vienna, 1946. p.29: A Letter Home, 1944. p.30: Sweet Dreams, 1957. p.33: Stranger On The Shore, 1953. p.34: Mothers' Day Surprise, 1955. p.37: Phoning A Friend, 1955. p.38: Post Card Perusal, 1953. p.41: Harrow Boy, 1951. p.42: Fireside Mail, circa 1955, © Lambert/Getty Images. p.44: I'll Have This One, 1951. p.47: Family Photos, circa 1955. p.48: Reflections, 1929. p.51: As cover. 1955. p.52: Letter Writer, 1938. p.55: Staying Behind, 1952. p.56: Wave Goodbye, circa 1955, © Lambert/Getty Images. p.58: The Kiss, 1955. p.61: Telephone Snacks, circa 1955, © John Zavisho/Getty Images. p.63: Missing You, 1956. p.64: Seaside Holiday, 1951. p.66: Mourning A Friend, 1937. p.69: Railway Fashion Shoot, 1950. p.70: Dear Mr Hixson, circa 1952, © Lambert/Getty Images. p.73: Train Window, 1948. p.75: Salisbury Cloisters, circa 1950. p.76: Crystal Gazing, 1953. p.79: Bolshoi Brit, 1959. p.81: Mothers Day, circa 1948. p.82: Titfield Thunderbolt, 1952. p.84: Pick Up The Phone, circa 1950. p.87: News From Home, 1950. p.88: Painting Of A Girl, circa 1938. p.90: Pixie Hood Pigtail, 1962. p.93: Dear John, 1956. p.94: Mud Flats, 1948. p.97: Looking At Brando, 1955. p.98: Old Man And The Sea, circa 1965, © Lambert/Getty Images. p.101: Memories, circa 1945, © Lambert/Getty Images. p.102: Looking Up, 1955. p.104: With Me Always, 1936. p.107: Pigeons, circa 1956.

Text Credits

p.13: Excerpt by Phyllis Theroux, used by kind permission of the author. p.17: Excerpt by Frederick Buechner, used by kind permission of the author. p.22: Excerpt from *Raising Demons* by Shirley Jackson, published by Academy Chicago Publishers, 1994. p.40: Excerpt from *Animal Farm* by George Orwell, originally published by Harcourt Brace Jovanovich, Inc, © 1946 by Harcourt Brace Jovanovich, Inc. p.45: Excerpt from *The House At Pooh Corner* by A.A. Milne, illustrations by E.H. Shephard, © 1928 by E.P. Dutton, renewed © 1956 by A.A. Milne. Used by permission of Dutton Children's Books, A division of Penguin Young Readers Group, A Member of Penguin Group (USA). Also used by permission of Egmont Books Ltd, London, © under the Berne convention. p.59: "The Look" by Sara Teasdale by permission of Wellesley College. p.65: Excerpt from "The Road Goes On Forever" by Robert Earl Keen Jr. Used by permission of Music Sales Ltd. p.67: Excerpt from *The Prophet,* by Kahlil Gibran, published by Random House, 2001. p.86: Excerpt by Richard Bach, used by permission of Scribner, a division of Simon & Schuster. p.92: Excerpt by Svetlana Alliluyeva, used by permission of The Alliluyeva Trust. p.99: Excerpt by Ray Bradbury, used by permission of Don Congdon Associates, Inc. All rights reserved. p.105: Excerpt from "i like my body when it is with your body" from *Complete Poems 1904-1962,* by E.E.Cummings, edited by George J. Firmage. Used by permission of W.W. Norton & Company Ltd. © 1991 by the Trustees for the E.E. Cummings Trust and George James Firmage.

Note: Every effort has been made to contact current copyright holders. Any omission is unintentional and the publisher would be pleased to hear from any copyright holders not acknowledged above.

Published by MQ Publications Limited

12 The Ivories, 6–8 Northampton Street, London, N1 2HY

Tel: + 44 (0)20 7359 2244   Fax: + 44 (0)20 7359 1616

e-mail: mail@mqpublications.com

website: www.mqpublications.com

ISBN: 1-84072-481-1

3 5 7 9 0 8 6 4 2

Text compilation: Wynn Wheldon

Printed and bound in China